Contents

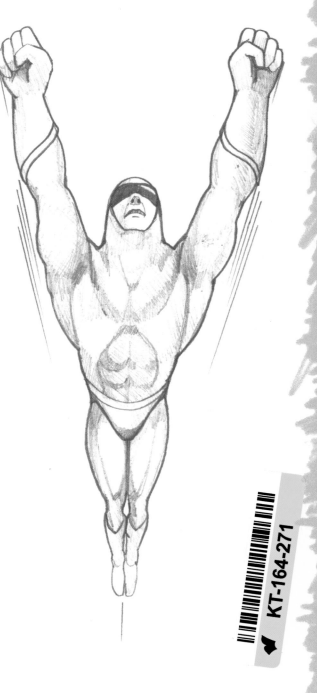

Making a start

Learning to draw is about looking and seeing. Keep practising and get to know your subject. Use a sketchbook to make quick drawings. Start by doodling and experimenting with shapes and patterns. There are many ways to draw but this book shows only some methods. Visit art galleries, look at artists' drawings and see how your friends draw, but above all, find your own way.

You can practise drawing figures using an artist's model — a wooden figure that can be put into various poses.

When drawing from photos, use construction lines to help you to understand the form of the body and how each of its parts relate to each other.

4

HOW TO DRAW
COMIC BOOK
HEROES

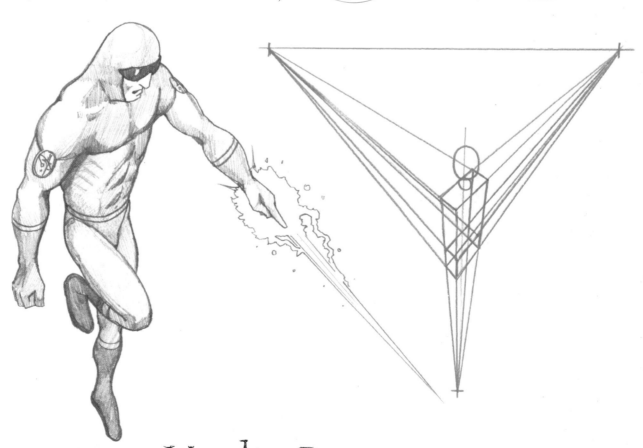

Mark Bergin

BOOK HOUSE

SALARIYA

Published in Great Britain in MMX by
Book House, an imprint of
The Salariya Book Company Ltd
25 Marlborough Place, Brighton BN1 1UB

1 3 5 7 9 8 6 4 2

Please visit our website at **www.book-house.co.uk**
or go to **www.salariya.com** for **free** electronic versions of:
You Wouldn't Want to be an Egyptian Mummy!
You Wouldn't Want to be a Roman Gladiator!
You Wouldn't Want to be a Polar Explorer!
**You Wouldn't Want to sail on a 19th-Century
  Whaling Ship!**

Author: Mark Bergin was born in Hastings in 1961.
He studied at Eastbourne College of Art and has
specialised in historical reconstructions as well as
aviation and maritime subjects since 1983. He lives
in Bexhill-on-Sea with his wife and three children.

Editor: Rob Walker

PB ISBN: 978-1-907184-27-7

A CIP catalogue record for this
book is available from the
British Library.

Printed and bound in China.
Printed on paper from
sustainable sources.

**WARNING: Fixatives should be
used only under adult supervision.**

PAPER FROM
SUSTAINABLE
FORESTS

Practice sketching people
in everyday surroundings.
This will help you to draw
faster and train you to
capture the main elements
of a pose quickly.

Try sketching friends and
family at home.

You can create new
poses by drawing
simple stick figures.

Perspective

If you look at a figure from different viewpoints, you will see that whichever part is closest to you looks larger, and the part furthest away from you looks smallest. Drawing in perspective is a way of creating a feeling of depth – of suggesting three dimensions on a flat surface.

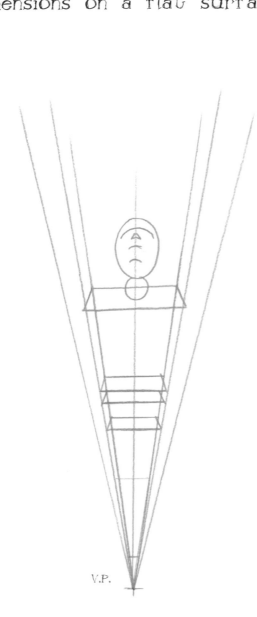

V.P.

The vanishing point (V.P.) is the place in a perspective drawing where parallel lines appear to meet. The position of the vanishing point depends on the viewer's eye level.

V.P.

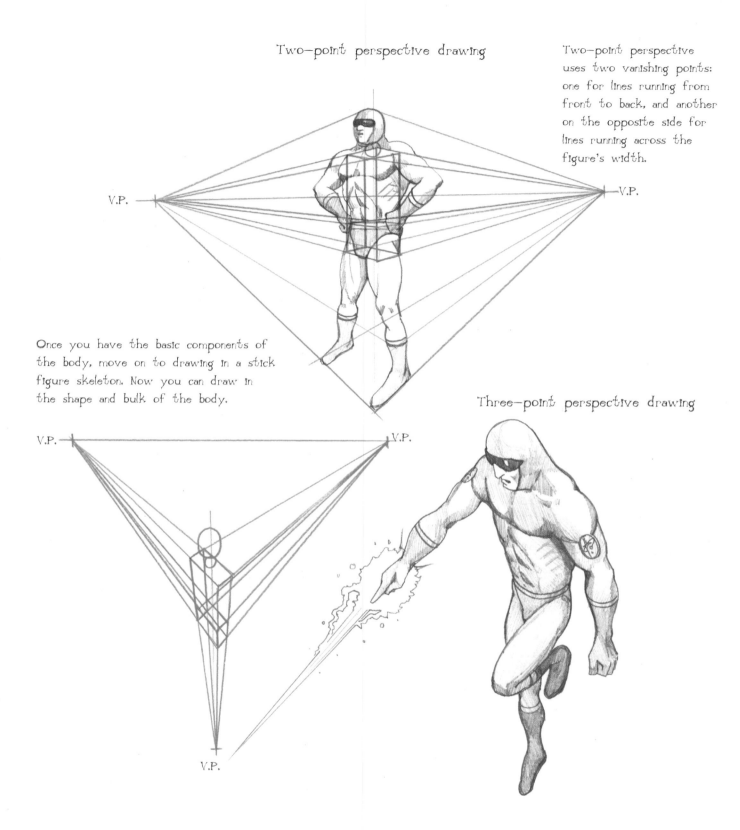

Two-point perspective drawing

Two-point perspective uses two vanishing points: one for lines running from front to back, and another on the opposite side for lines running across the figure's width.

V.P.

V.P.

Once you have the basic components of the body, move on to drawing in a stick figure skeleton. Now you can draw in the shape and bulk of the body.

V.P.

V.P.

Three-point perspective drawing

V.P.

Three-point perspective drawings use three vanishing points. This method is good for drawing objects at more dramatic angles.

V.P. = vanishing point

7

Drawing materials

Try using different types of drawing papers and materials. Experiment with charcoal, wax crayons and pastels. All pens, from felt-tips to ballpoints, will make interesting marks — try drawing with pen and ink on wet paper for a variety of results.

Silhouette is a style of drawing that uses only a solid black shadow.

Ink

Felt-tip

Charcoal is very soft and can be used for big, bold drawings. Ask an adult to spray your charcoal drawings with fixative to prevent smudging.

You can create special effects in a drawing done with **wax crayons** by scraping parts of the colour away.

8

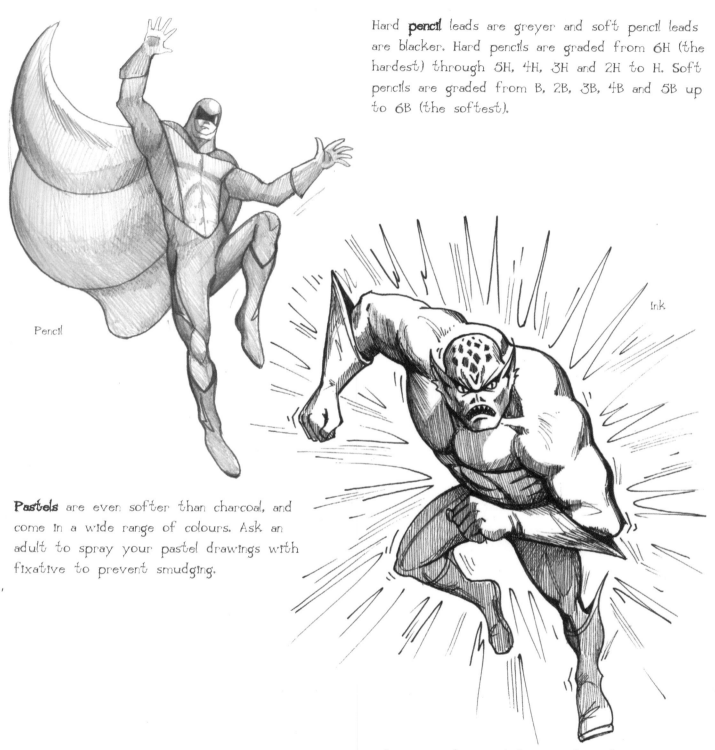

Hard **pencil** leads are greyer and soft pencil leads are blacker. Hard pencils are graded from 6H (the hardest) through 5H, 4H, 3H and 2H to H. Soft pencils are graded from B, 2B, 3B, 4B and 5B up to 6B (the softest).

Pencil

Ink

Pastels are even softer than charcoal, and come in a wide range of colours. Ask an adult to spray your pastel drawings with fixative to prevent smudging.

Lines drawn in ink cannot be erased, so keep your ink drawings sketchy and less rigid. Don't worry about mistakes as these lines can be lost in the drawing as it develops.

9

Flying super hero

The flying pose is a classic image of the super hero genre. The figure is often shown with an outstretched arm, clenched fist and usually a cape to add dynamism to the pose.

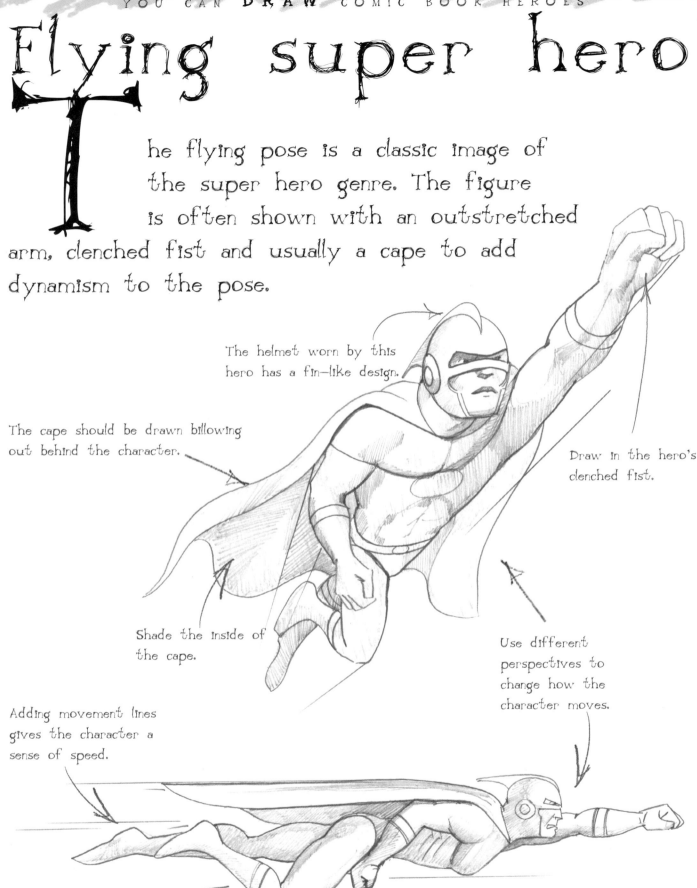

The helmet worn by this hero has a fin-like design.

The cape should be drawn billowing out behind the character.

Draw in the hero's clenched fist.

Shade the inside of the cape.

Use different perspectives to change how the character moves.

Adding movement lines gives the character a sense of speed.

10

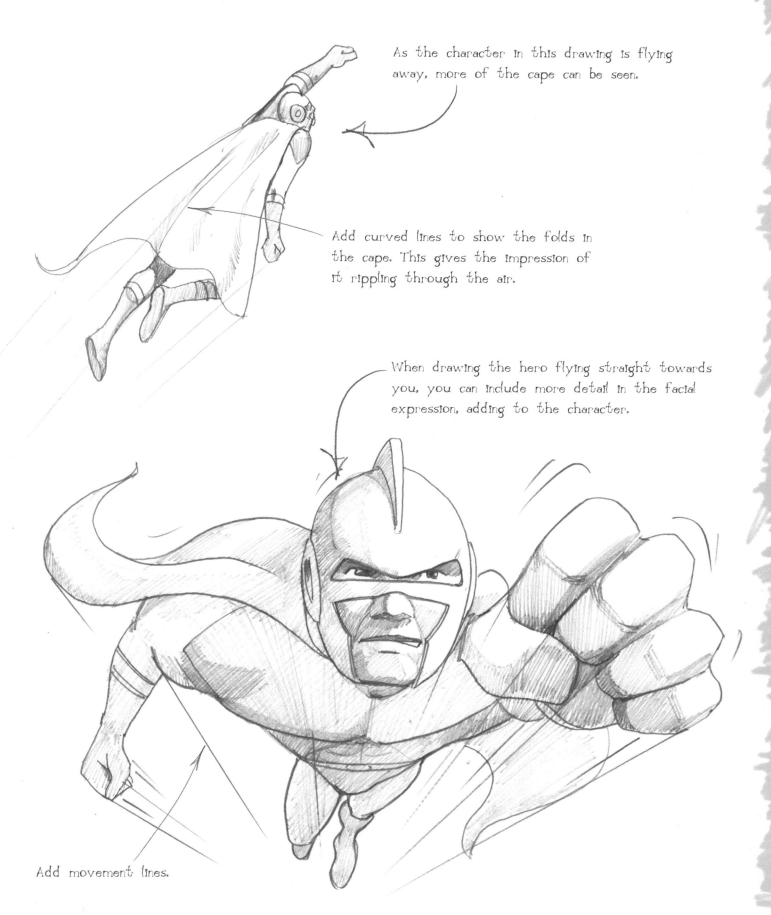

As the character in this drawing is flying away, more of the cape can be seen.

Add curved lines to show the folds in the cape. This gives the impression of it rippling through the air.

When drawing the hero flying straight towards you, you can include more detail in the facial expression, adding to the character.

Add movement lines.

Adapting characters

These simple figures can be adapted to become any costumed hero striking a heroic pose. Here they can be seen as spies, sci-fi warriors or super heroes.

Spies

Using the basic figure, draw in the hands, hair and facial details. Then add the details of the spies' costumes and accessories.

Draw the basic shape of the figures using simple lines and ovals.

Add hi-tech glasses and microphones

Draw a bag slung round the shoulder and hanging at waist level.

Draw in the belt with pouches.

Using curved lines draw a long coat on the lady spy.

Sci-fi warriors

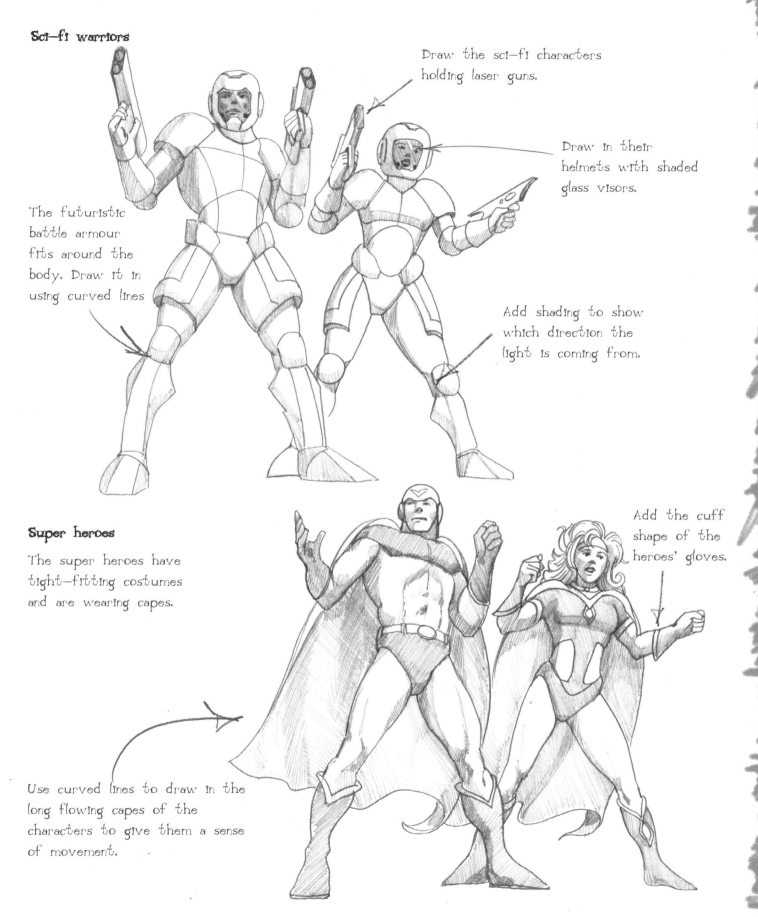

Draw the sci-fi characters holding laser guns.

Draw in their helmets with shaded glass visors.

The futuristic battle armour fits around the body. Draw it in using curved lines

Add shading to show which direction the light is coming from.

Super heroes

The super heroes have tight-fitting costumes and are wearing capes.

Add the cuff shape of the heroes' gloves.

Use curved lines to draw in the long flowing capes of the characters to give them a sense of movement.

Good vs bad

Here are some pretty evil character designs.

Every super hero needs a super villain to battle against! The details of a character's face and costume can instantly place them on the side of good or evil.

This set of super villains look ready to do evil. Note their rough and menacing appearance with torn, ragged capes and unfriendly looks.

The super heroes' looks are quite the opposite to that of the villains. They look clean and virtuous.

In this action scene the hero fights the villain. The villain's immense size helps to create a sense of intimidation and the scale of evil that must be overcome.

The hero is using his super powers to throw energy bolts at the villain.

Add in details like hair and bindings, and any costumes.

Try to capture the sense of movement in your drawings with the use of dramatic poses.

This dynamic pose shows the hero dealing out justice to a super villain scientist.

The strange circuit design on the villain's costume and test tube in his hand suggest he is a mad scientist.

Use perspective to add to the drama of the scene.

15

Running man

The running man uses his power of super speed to rescue those in peril and catch the villains.

Draw a straight line for the spine.

Head

Torso

Hips

Add three ovals: one each for the head, torso and hips. The torso oval is much longer.

Draw small circles for the shoulders.

Sketch in two cylinders to show the direction of the arms.

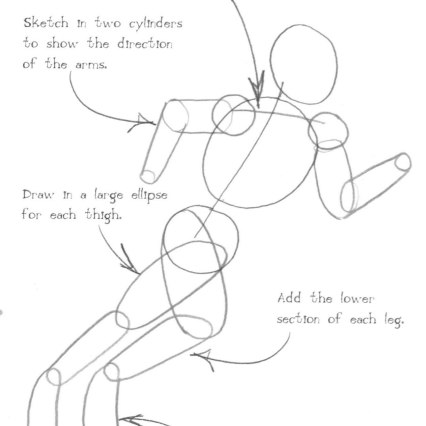

Draw in a large ellipse for each thigh.

Add the lower section of each leg.

Draw in the basic shape and direction of the feet.

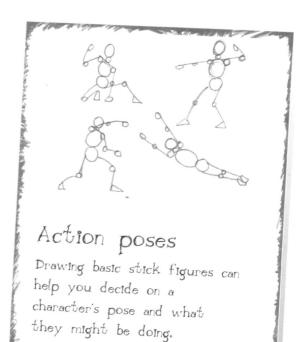

Action poses

Drawing basic stick figures can help you decide on a character's pose and what they might be doing.

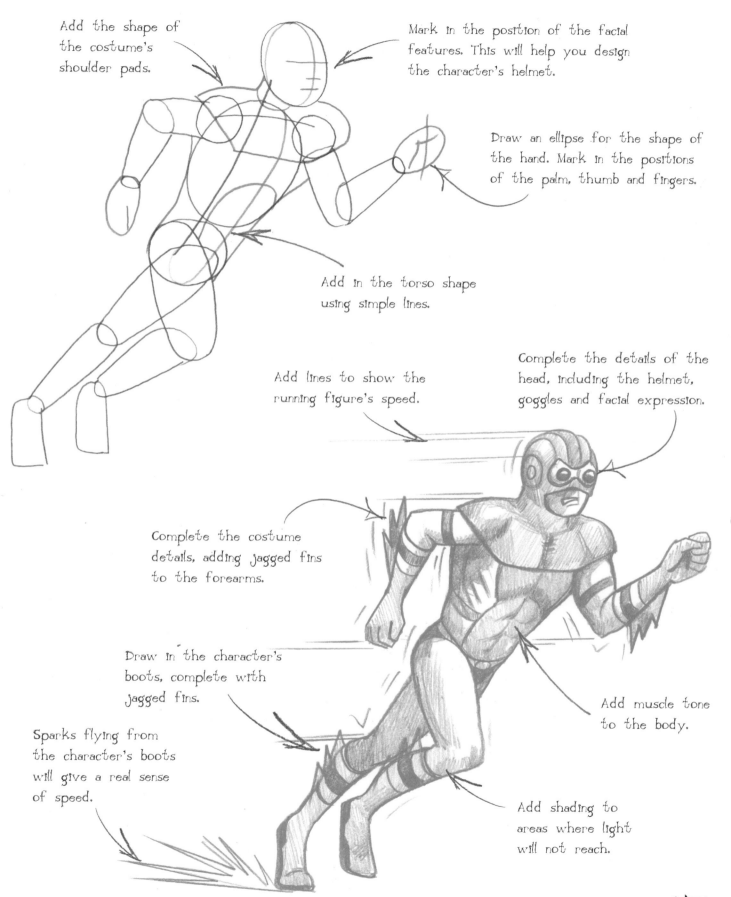

Add the shape of the costume's shoulder pads.

Mark in the position of the facial features. This will help you design the character's helmet.

Draw an ellipse for the shape of the hand. Mark in the positions of the palm, thumb and fingers.

Add in the torso shape using simple lines.

Add lines to show the running figure's speed.

Complete the details of the head, including the helmet, goggles and facial expression.

Complete the costume details, adding jagged fins to the forearms.

Draw in the character's boots, complete with jagged fins.

Add muscle tone to the body.

Sparks flying from the character's boots will give a real sense of speed.

Add shading to areas where light will not reach.

17

Super-strong man

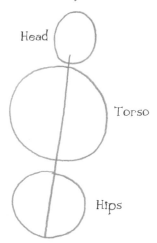

Super-strength is a trait often found in super heroes. This character fights evil using his strength to overcome all odds. Here he can be seen lifting a huge boulder over his head.

Draw in a straight line for the character's spine.

Head

Torso

Hips

Add three circles for the head, torso and hips. Make the torso shape larger.

Add a small circle for each shoulder.

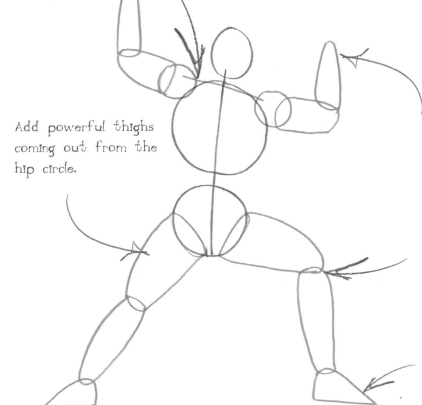

Add powerful thighs coming out from the hip circle.

Draw cylindrical shapes for the position of each arm.

Draw in the shape of the lower legs, overlapping them with the thighs where the knee joints would be.

Sketch in the basic shape and direction of the feet.

Draw a teardrop shape for each hand, remembering to think about how the hands would grasp the boulder.

Mark the position of the facial features.

Draw in the basic shape of the figure's torso.

Draw in a large, rugged boulder.

Give your drawing added action by adding small fragments of rock falling off the boulder.

Draw a large shadow under the hero, as the huge boulder casts a shadow too.

Complete the details of the hero's face and torso. Make sure he has a well-defined muscle structure under his costume.

19

Hi-tech spy

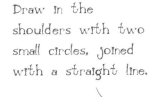

The hi-tech spy lives in the dangerous and exciting world of espionage. She needs all the latest equipment and technology to stay on top and survive.

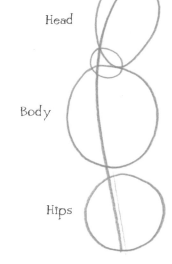

Head

Body

Hips

Draw in four ellipses, one each for the head, neck, body and hips.

Draw in the shoulders with two small circles, joined with a straight line.

Sketch in the position of the facial features.

Draw in the legs of the spy.

Overlap both sections of each leg to indicate the joints.

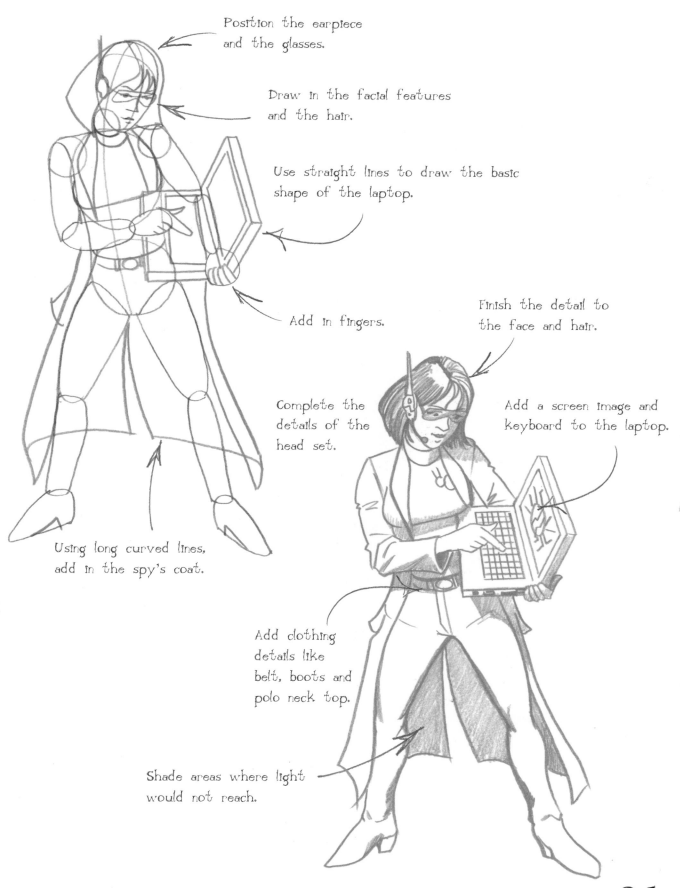

Position the earpiece and the glasses.

Draw in the facial features and the hair.

Use straight lines to draw the basic shape of the laptop.

Finish the detail to the face and hair.

Add in fingers.

Complete the details of the head set.

Add a screen image and keyboard to the laptop.

Using long curved lines, add in the spy's coat.

Add clothing details like belt, boots and polo neck top.

Shade areas where light would not reach.

21

Mutant figure

The mutant figure can be anything you can imagine. The figure here is a wolf—man crouching on all fours, ready to attack!

Draw circles for the hips, body, neck and head.

Hips

Neck

Head

Body

Draw two circles for the shoulders and connect them underneath with a straight line.

Sketch overlapping ellipses to create the legs.

Sketch in the position of the feet.

Each arm is formed with two ellipses, a smaller one overlapping a larger one where they join.

Draw a large circle for each hand.

Mutant Heads

These mutant heads will give you some ideas for creating your own mutants!

Sketch in small jagged lines around the outlines of the wolf—man to indicate fur.

Draw in two curved lines for the tail.

Add claw shapes to the back feet.

Sketch in the basic facial features.

Add v-shaped ears to the head.

Draw in the wolf—man's sharp, pointed claws.

Complete the feet details.

Draw small overlapping lines to create the look of fur.

Draw in the wolf—man's leather harness.

Finish all the facial details.

Sci-fi warrior

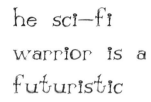

The sci-fi warrior is a futuristic soldier with technologically-advanced armour and weaponry for fighting in the furthest reaches of the galaxy.

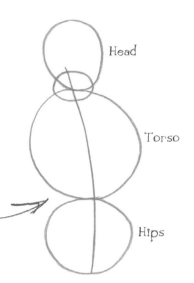

Head

Torso

Hips

Start by drawing four ellipses: one each for the head, neck, torso and hips. Add a curved centre line.

Add two small circles on either side of the torso.

Add an oval to each arm for the hands.

Draw a line to position the laser gun.

Sketch in the position of the arms with simple shapes that overlap at the joints.

Add curved lines for the top part of each leg.

Add straight lines for the lower part of each leg.

Draw in the shape and direction of the feet.

24

Use construction lines as a guide to draw in the basic shape and details of a helmet.

Draw the shape of the laser gun using straight lines.

Roughly sketch in the shape of the fingers.

Add the jet pack on his back.

Add the body armour. Draw lines to indicate the joints in it.

Complete the details of the face and helmet.

Details like this circuit board can give the drawing a more futuristic look.

Draw sharp spiky lines coming out of the end of the gun to create a dramatic effect.

Shade in areas where light would not reach.

Complete the details of the armour. All the shapes should be very precise.

Jungle explorer

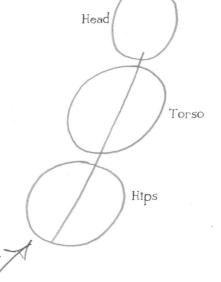

An expedition into the jungle can be very hazardous so the explorer has to be ready for action. In this drawing the explorer is swinging from a rope.

Head

Torso

Hips

Draw in a centre line for the spine and add three circles for the head, torso and hips.

Draw two circles connected by a line for the shoulders.

Add rounded shapes for the arms that overlap at the shoulder and elbow joints.

Sketch in larger rounded shapes for the thighs.

Draw the lower legs with a simple tube shape, overlapping the top part of the leg to position the knee joints.

Draw two curved lines
for the rope.

Draw the basic shape
of hands clinging to
the rope.

Mark in the position
of the facial features.

Use curved lines to
create movement in the
shape of the hair.

Sketch in the
shape of the chest.

Finish the
facial details.

Draw lines across
the rope to make
it look real.

Add a sheathed
knife strapped to
the belt.

Draw in the character's boots. Show
the sole of the boot coming
towards you. Remember to use
perspective to proportion the boot.

Add the detail of the
clothing: top, socks, belt,
shorts and pockets.

Add a few
movement lines.

27

Cyborg

A cyborg is a combination of man and machine! With its mechanical additions the cyborg is far faster and stronger than a normal human being.

Head

Torso

Hips

Draw in simple shapes for the head, torso and hips with a curved line for the spine. Add a line for the direction of the shoulders.

Sketch in construction lines to give shape and direction to the head.

Draw an oval for the hand.

Extend the direction of the shoulder line forward. Now draw in a long tube using perspective for the outstretched cybernetic arm.

Draw rounded overlapping shapes for the legs.

Add the shape and direction of each foot.

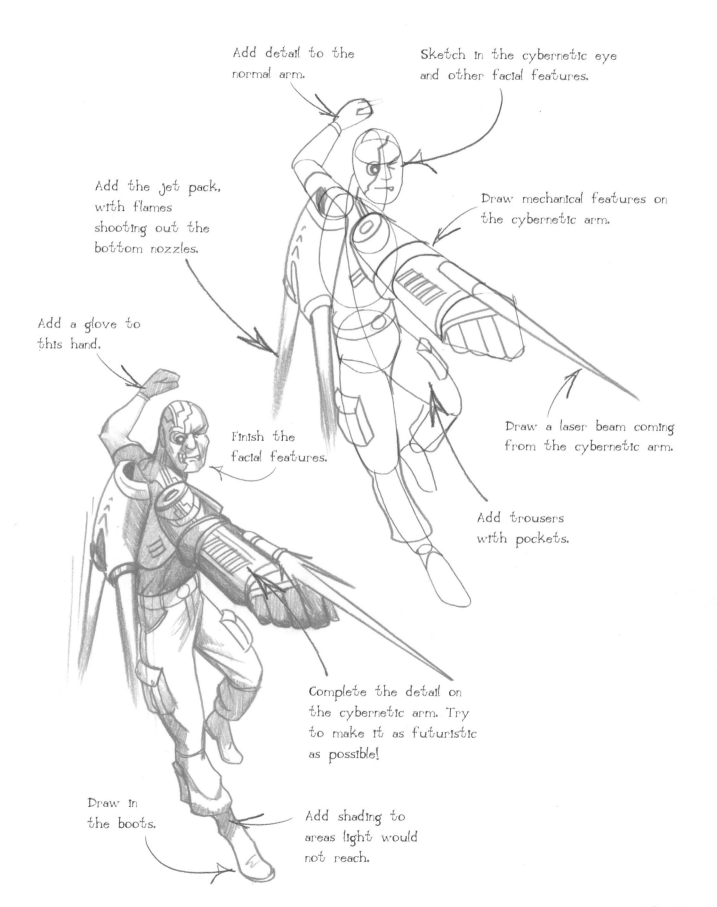

Add detail to the
normal arm.

Sketch in the cybernetic eye
and other facial features.

Add the jet pack,
with flames
shooting out the
bottom nozzles.

Draw mechanical features on
the cybernetic arm.

Add a glove to
this hand.

Finish the
facial features.

Draw a laser beam coming
from the cybernetic arm.

Add trousers
with pockets.

Complete the detail on
the cybernetic arm. Try
to make it as futuristic
as possible!

Draw in
the boots.

Add shading to
areas light would
not reach.

29

Martial arts warrior

The martial arts warrior defeats his foes using only his strength and his martial arts fighting technique. In this dramatic and action-filled pose he is performing a flying kick.

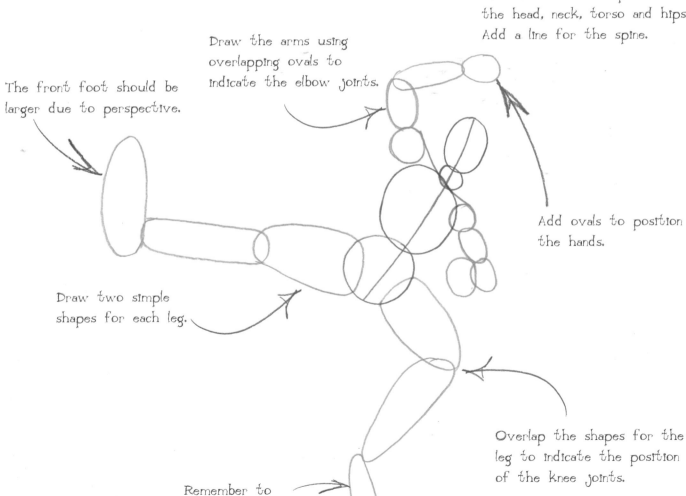

Draw in rounded shapes for the head, neck, torso and hips. Add a line for the spine.

Head

Torso

Hips

Draw the arms using overlapping ovals to indicate the elbow joints.

The front foot should be larger due to perspective.

Add ovals to position the hands.

Draw two simple shapes for each leg.

Overlap the shapes for the leg to indicate the position of the knee joints.

Remember to make the back foot smaller.